D1174827

12 TIPS TO MAINTAIN
BRAIN HEALTH

by Maddie Spalding

www.12StoryLibrary.com

Copyright © 2017 by Peterson Publishing Company, North Mankato, MN 56003. All rights reserved. No part of this book may be reproduced or utilized in any form or by any means without written permission from the publisher.

12-Story Library is an imprint of Peterson Publishing Company and Press Room Editions.

Produced for 12-Story Library by Red Line Editorial

Photographs ©: Arieliona/Shutterstock Images, cover, 1; Syda Productions/Dreamstime, 4; FernandoAH/iStockphoto, 5; savageultralight/iStockphoto, 6, 29; monkeybusinessimages/iStockphoto, 7; digitalskillet/iStockphoto, 8; Art-Of-Photo/iStockphoto, 9; Air Images/Shutterstock Images, 10; Peter Schneider/Keystone/AP Images, 11; MarkHatfield/iStockphoto, 12; YinYang/iStockphoto, 13; Tsuji/iStockphoto, 14; ejwhite/iStockphoto, 15; Dragonimages/iStockphoto, 16, 28; skynesher/iStockphoto, 17; PeopleImages/iStockphoto, 18, 20; Christopher Futcher/iStockphoto, 19; jarenwicklund/iStockphoto, 21; Tashi-Delek/iStockphoto, 22; Prasit Rodphan/Shutterstock Images, 23; visionchina/iStockphoto, 24; Orren Jack Turner/Library of Congress, 25; Monkey Business Images/Shutterstock Images, 26; jane/iStockphoto, 27

Library of Congress Cataloging-in-Publication Data
Names: Spalding, Maddie, 1990- author.
Title: 12 tips to maintain brain health / by Maddie Spalding.
Description: Mankato, MN : 12-Story Library, [2017] | Series: Healthy living
  | Audience: Grades 4-6. | Includes bibliographical references and index.
Identifiers: LCCN 2016007443 (print) | LCCN 2016011457 (ebook) | ISBN
  9781632353689 (library bound : alk. paper) | ISBN 9781632353863 (pbk. :
  alk. paper) | ISBN 9781621435105 (hosted ebook)
Subjects: LCSH: Brain--Juvenile literature. | Brain--Care and
  hygiene--Juvenile literature. | Mental health--Juvenile literature. |
  Thought and thinking--Juvenile literature.
Classification: LCC QP376 .S735 2017 (print) | LCC QP376 (ebook) | DDC
  612.8/2--dc23
LC record available at http://lccn.loc.gov/2016007443

Printed in the United States of America
Mankato, MN
May, 2016

Access free, up-to-date content on this topic plus a full digital version of this book. Scan the QR code on page 31 or use your school's login at 12StoryLibrary.com.

Table of Contents

Exercise to Improve Brain Blood Flow

People exercise for different reasons. Many people focus on physical reasons. They may exercise to lose weight or build muscle. Physical exercise also has mental benefits.

Your heart pumps faster when you exercise. Exercise increases blood flow to all parts of your body. This includes your brain. Blood delivers oxygen to brain cells. More oxygen means more energy. You may feel like you are able to think more clearly after exercise. This is because the increase in blood flow energizes your brain.

Exercising the body is a great way to energize the brain.

Aerobic exercises, such as running, improve blood flow to your brain.

Your brain also releases endorphins when you exercise. These are feel-good chemicals. Endorphins give you energy. They lift you out of a bad mood. Your mood affects your memory. Being in a good mood helps you stay focused and alert. So it might be best to study for a test after running or playing your favorite sport.

Many kinds of exercise have this effect on your brain. This includes sports such as tennis, which requires coordination. Aerobic exercises also have this effect.

Exercise doesn't have to be intense. Even walking for a half hour a day can give your brain these benefits.

1

Hours of exercise per day recommended for people ages 6 to 17.

- Exercise increases blood flow.
- Blood delivers oxygen to your brain.
- Increased energy and endorphins boost your mood and memory.

2

Socialize with Friends and Family

Think about the people you talk to every day. These people might be friends or family. You may talk to them for many reasons. Maybe they are good listeners. Maybe they offer you support or advice. There is one more reason you can add to your list. Talking to others benefits your brain.

Part of your brain is activated when you socialize. It is called the amygdala. This part stores memories. It also helps you process emotions. Your brain recalls and retains information as you talk with others.

Exchanging ideas with other people can also help you solve problems.

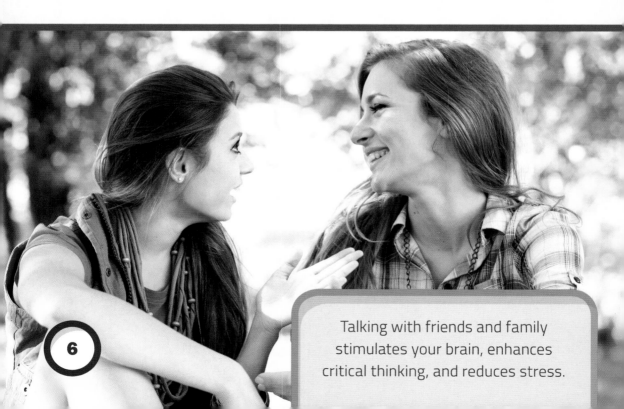

Talking with friends and family stimulates your brain, enhances critical thinking, and reduces stress.

4.5

Approximate average number of hours a US high school student spends with friends and family on a weekday.

- Socializing can improve your memory.
- You can gain new knowledge by talking to others.
- Socializing reduces stress.
- You exercise critical thinking skills when talking to others.

SOCIALIZING IN THE DIGITAL WORLD

By age two, children learn to communicate by observing what they see and hear. They start to communicate in new ways as they grow up. Many American children get their first cell phone when they are quite young. Communicating this way can have a negative impact. Talking face to face is better. Face-to-face communication can help you better understand emotions. It allows you to read facial expressions.

You may learn new information or be introduced to new ideas. Having a good discussion with others involves critical thinking. Your knowledge and critical thinking skills can improve as you talk with others.

Having social support can also help get you through tough situations. Stress can have bad effects on overall brain health if it goes unmanaged. Engaging in good conversation can help you reduce and manage stress.

Try substituting screen time with face-to-face communication with friends.

3

Sleep to Keep Your Brain Sharp

Exercise benefits your brain, but rest is just as important. Rest keeps your brain healthy. As you sleep, your brain is hard at work. Some parts are actually more active when you are asleep.

A lot can happen in one day. Maybe you studied for a big test. You also probably came across new sights, smells, or sounds. Your brain gets more information each day than it can possibly process. Sleeping gives your brain a chance to process it all.

There are five sleep stages. Brain waves slow in the first four stages. You enter into deeper sleep at each stage. Your brain becomes highly active in the last stage. This stage

Getting good sleep at night helps your brain process the day's thoughts and interactions.

Try sleeping away from your phone at night to get better sleep.

is called rapid eye movement (REM) sleep. Your eyes dart around and your heart beats faster. You start to dream.

All this movement during REM sleep sounds opposite of a good night's rest. But REM sleep benefits your brain the most. When you dream, messages are shared between brain cells. This helps your brain form memories. Not getting enough sleep can impact your memory. Exhaustion can also make it difficult for you to concentrate.

9-11
The hours of sleep the National Sleep Foundation recommends for people aged 6 to 13.

- Your brain processes information as you sleep.
- Memories are formed during the REM stage of the sleep cycle.
- Getting a good night's sleep makes you alert the next day.

THINK ABOUT IT

Compare your sleep habits to the recommended sleep guidelines. Are you getting enough sleep at night? If not, what may be interfering with your sleep schedule?

4

Keep Your Mind Fit with Mental Activities

Mental activities are great ways to exercise your brain. Mental activity is as important as physical activity in keeping your brain healthy. You probably exercise your brain a lot during the school day. There are also many kinds of fun mental activities to do outside of school.

The best mental activities for your brain are those that are challenging but enjoyable. These activities can build neuron connections in your brain. Neuron connections become stronger when you do mental activities.

Challenge a friend to a game of chess to exercise your brain and hone your reasoning skills.

Along with being a top chess player, Judit Polgár is also one of the world's smartest people.

Many mental activities benefit your brain. Board games such as Scrabble and Monopoly exercise your reasoning skills. Strategy games such as chess also exercise your brain. Puzzles and word searches are another option. They require creative thinking. These activities may help you recognize patterns and think outside the box.

100 billion
Average number of neurons in a human brain.

- Mental activities exercise your brain.
- The best mental activities for your brain are those that are difficult but still fun.
- Strategy and reasoning games can help you think more creatively.

CHESS GENIUS JUDIT POLGÁR

Judit Polgár is a top chess player and one of the world's smartest people. Her father taught her chess. She now teaches children chess to help them develop problem-solving skills. She says that "the activities on the chessboard develop logical thinking, creativity, acceptance of winning and losing."

5

Take a Break from Multitasking

Multitasking involves quickly switching from one task to another. Maybe you keep your phone nearby to text friends as you study. Whatever form it comes in, multitasking often is not good for your brain.

Multitasking divides your attention. You need to make decisions involving all tasks. These may be small decisions, such as how to respond to a text. But making even small decisions can take a lot of brain energy. Facing many decisions at once can make you feel stressed. When stressed, your body produces adrenaline. This hormone increases your heart rate. It causes your muscles to tighten. Being in

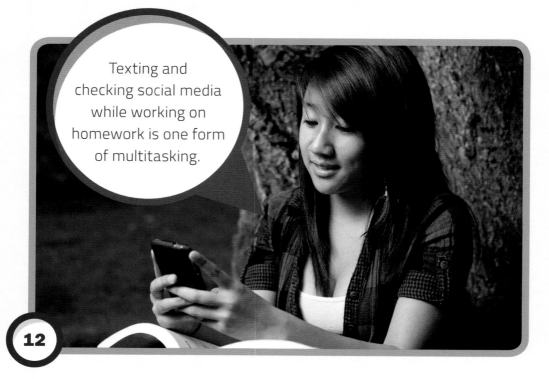

Texting and checking social media while working on homework is one form of multitasking.

Yoga is one form of meditation you can take part in to lower your stress levels.

this state of stress for a long time is not good for your brain. You may find it difficult to concentrate. You may have trouble remembering information.

New information can go to the wrong part of your brain when you multitask. Try studying without any distractions. This allows new information to go to the hippocampus. This is the part of the brain that stores ideas. The information will be much easier for you to recall if it is in your hippocampus.

20
Minutes of meditation recommended per day.

- Multitasking can make you feel stressed.
- You may have difficulty focusing and remembering information when you multitask.
- Meditation can reduce stress and improve concentration.

Some people use meditation to lower their stress levels. Meditation improves concentration and reduces stress. Taking time out of your day to remove yourself from distractions can benefit your brain.

Eat Healthy Foods to Boost Brainpower

Your brain needs energy to function. The foods you eat fuel your body. They also boost your brainpower. Choosing nutrient-rich foods is an important step in keeping your brain healthy.

Your parents may tell you to eat vegetables or fruit. Maybe they tell you that eating spinach will make you stronger. Or maybe they say eating carrots will make your eyesight better. There is some truth to these suggestions. But fruits and vegetables don't just benefit your body. They can also benefit your brain. Vegetables such as broccoli and spinach are high in vitamin K. Vitamin K boosts brainpower.

Plenty of other foods benefit your brain the same way. Beans and whole grains have glucose. Your brain needs this for energy. Glucose

Brain-healthy foods, such as blueberries, can improve your memory and learning ability.

Opt for milk instead of an energy drink when thirsty.

is released into your bloodstream. This keeps your brain alert all day. Cereal and oatmeal are good sources of whole grain. Nuts and meat, such as beef and chicken, are high in zinc. Zinc improves your memory and thinking skills. Your brain also needs omega-3 essential fatty acids to work well. Fish and eggs are good sources of this. Eating a variety of these kinds of foods is a good way to keep your brain healthy.

1 ½
Cups of fruit recommended per day for people aged 9 to 13.

- Certain foods provide glucose, giving your brain energy.
- Vitamins and minerals that are good for your brain include vitamin K and zinc.
- Eating a variety of nutrient-rich foods is a good way to maintain overall brain health.

BRAIN-BOOSTING BEVERAGES

Many popular sodas and energy drinks contain a lot of sugar. Your brain produces chemicals that help with learning and memory. However, consuming high levels of sugar interferes with the production of these chemicals. Swapping sodas and energy drinks for a beverage high in nutrients, such as milk, is better for your brain.

15

Get Creative

It is said that the right side of your brain is responsible for creativity. But creative activities use parts of both your left and right brain. Making creativity a habit can boost brain health by exercising these areas of your brain.

Playing a musical instrument is a popular creative activity. Musicians are better at learning a language than non-musicians. They are better able to pick up on small differences in syllables and sounds. Other creative activities, such as drawing and writing, use your imagination. Using your imagination activates parts of your brain involved in understanding other people. Imaginative people are able to more easily consider what other people may be thinking and feeling. Your brain also releases feel-good chemicals when you do something creative. These chemicals can improve memory and reduce stress.

Some people are more creative than others. But creativity is something that can be practiced. You don't have to be an expert in the activity you choose. You

Just listening to music activates parts of the left and right brain involved in processing speech.

THINK ABOUT IT

What kinds of creative activities do you normally do? How do these activities benefit your brain? Think about other creative activities that would have positive effects on your brain.

20

Percentage of your body's energy that your brain uses.

- Creative activities exercise many parts of your brain.
- Playing music regularly can improve your ability to learn new languages.
- Using your imagination may allow you to better understand other people.
- Even small creative activities can benefit your brain.

could try a creative hobby such as a scrapbooking. Even daydreaming or imagining future events can benefit your brain.

Gardening is a creative hobby you can do with friends or family.

17

Explore New Activities

Think about the last new skill you learned. Maybe it was hard at first. Maybe you found it frustrating. But did you feel a sense of accomplishment after you mastered it? Learning a new skill or activity challenges your brain. Working on a new skill takes more brain functioning because your brain doesn't know it yet. Your brain stores new information that you retrieve when you work on the skill. Learning a new skill improves your memory this way.

To get these brain benefits, choose a skill a little outside of your comfort zone. A skill that is too challenging might not end up being enjoyable. It might leave you

Learning to play an instrument is one way to explore a new activity and exercise your brain.

feeling stressed. This is not good for your brain health. You should be able to find a flow while working on the new activity. Flow happens when you are fully concentrated on an activity that is challenging but fun. People learn information best when they are in a state of flow.

Many skills and activities can have these brain benefits. Learning a new language or how to play a musical instrument are excellent skills to maintain your brain health. The skill you learn does not need to be this complex. You might try learn a new computer skill. Learning even small skills can benefit your brain.

Try learning a new language with a friend.

1,000
Average total hours of practice it takes to master a new language.

- Learning a new skill can improve your memory.
- The new skill or activity you choose should be challenging but fun.
- You should aim to achieve a state of flow when working on your new skill.

LEARNING LANGUAGES

The human brain can learn many languages. People who learn more than one language are better at tuning out unnecessary words and information. Learning a second language hard-wires your brain to more easily learn a future language.

Keep Organized

Your mind is flooded with new information every day. Some of this information is unnecessary. For example, you do not need to remember the outfit of every single person you see on a given day. Other information, such as what you learn in class, is important. Your mind will need to store and easily recall this information. Your short-term memory can only hold so much information.

Approximately only seven pieces of information can be stored in

Writing down information and keeping it organized can help you commit information to memory.

short-term memory at one time. Information stays in your short-term memory for 15 to 30 seconds. Then one of two things happens. The information is either forgotten or put in your long-term memory. The key to keeping information in long-term memory is to recall it often. Use memory recall tricks to retrieve it. These tricks can be key words or phrases that help you remember the information.

There are many methods to improve your long-term memory. Write organized notes on a topic. Writing them out can help you better remember come test time. You can separate information under headers. You could use a person's name as a header if you are learning about important people in history. Jot down the key information. Summarize information in your own words. Using these techniques will make it easy to study and remember information.

> Try writing down key facts on notecards for a different way to study.

501
World record for the most digits in the right order memorized in five minutes.

- New information is either forgotten or transferred into long-term memory.
- Organizing information can help you commit it to long-term memory.
- Explore new organizational skills and study techniques to improve your memory.

Seek Out Quiet Learning Environments

Adopting good study skills is one way to boost your memory. There are further steps you can take to improve your memory. Your learning environment, or where you study, determines how much you will remember.

Studies have shown that background noise, such as talking and music, affects concentration. It can be hard to study in places where background noise is even low. It can be hard to focus on what you are trying to study. You may start to

Background noises are very low in libraries, making libraries great places to study.

feel stressed. Stress interferes with learning and memory.

A quiet environment helps you focus. Quiet is great when you are working on a detailed task. But quiet environments are not always best for your brain. Environments with low to moderate levels of background noise can help when you are working on a creative project. This is because creativity does not require as much focused attention as studying. Some background noise stimulates your brain. It makes it easier for you to think creatively. Yet there is still a limit on how much background noise your brain can handle. Too much noise will make it difficult for you to think.

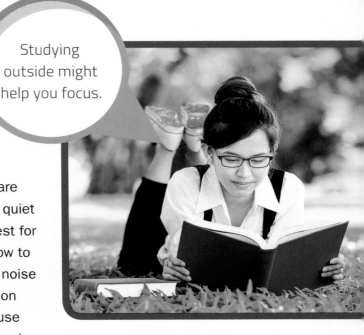

Studying outside might help you focus.

28
Percentage of US students in grades three through six who are often stressed out by homework.

- Where you choose to study affects how much information you will remember.
- Background noise affects your ability to concentrate and memorize information.
- Some background noise can benefit your brain when you are working on a creative project.

THINK ABOUT IT

Think of places where you have studied or worked on projects. Which environments made you feel the most productive? Why might this be the case?

23

Use Your Senses

Think of your most vivid memory. What sights and sounds do you remember? Can you recall any tastes or smells? Memories linked with sensory details are the easiest to remember.

Learning new information is easiest when you use more than one of your five senses. Each sense corresponds to a different part of your brain. The more senses you use to learn information, the more your brain is engaged. Listening to a teacher engages your sense of hearing. Using more senses to learn this information will help you better remember it. You could draw a concept of what you learn. Or you could look up pictures online. Viewing pictures of what you are learning about will help you better remember it.

There may also be ways to use your sense of smell, taste, or touch while you study. You could do some role-playing if you are studying history. Imagine yourself as someone in that time period. Imagine what they may have

How could your sense of smell help you remember something?

ALBERT EINSTEIN'S THOUGHT EXPERIMENTS

Famous scientist Albert Einstein often came up with new theories using thought experiments. Einstein did regular lab experiments. But he would often imagine the concept in his head as a thought experiment before doing a regular experiment. When he was 16, he imagined himself riding a wave of light next to other waves of light. Using visualization as well as hands-on learning in the lab, Einstein discovered new concepts in science.

smelled, tasted, or touched. Maybe you are studying a scientific theory. Doing some hands-on experiments in the classroom may help you to better remember that theory.

13

Milliseconds it takes for your brain to identify an image after seeing the image.

- Each of your five senses corresponds to a different part of your brain.
- The more senses you use to learn information, the more your brain learns.
- Using sensory-learning techniques can boost your memory.

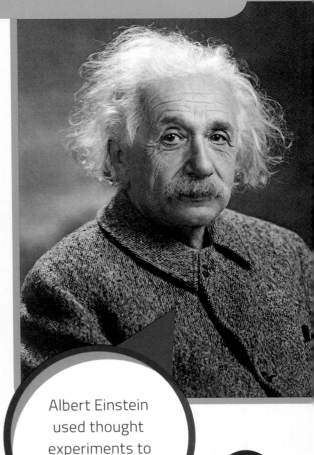

Albert Einstein used thought experiments to discover scientific concepts.

Keep a Journal

Journaling can be a way to relax at the end of the day. It can also be a good way to remember details you would otherwise forget. Whatever your reason, journaling is a good habit for your brain.

Journaling is a form of free writing. There are no rules. This kind of free writing helps you process thoughts and emotions. Stressful experiences of the day may be hard to put into words. But writing about them can help you sort through them. Writing this way can help relieve some stress. Getting rid of some of your stress before bed will help you sleep better.

Free writing in the form of journaling allows you to write and draw whatever comes to mind.

Jot down main events throughout your day and write more about them later.

Journaling has many other brain benefits. It can improve your memory and boost your intelligence. You may search for new words and expand your vocabulary as you write. Your emotional intelligence will improve as well. This is measured by your ability to understand your and others' emotions. Understanding yourself and others may also help you better communicate with others.

Keeping to a regular journaling schedule helps you practice self-discipline. Self-discipline is a trait you need to develop habits. Once you make journaling a habit, other healthy habits may follow. You may start to develop a regular sleep schedule. This will help you get enough sleep each night. You may start to make eating nutrient-rich brain foods a habit. Or you might start to exercise regularly. Journaling can be a gateway to other habits that also boost your brain health.

15
Minutes of journaling per day recommended to maintain brain health.

- Journaling regularly can relieve stress.
- Journaling can improve memory.
- Making journaling a habit can improve your self-discipline.

Fact Sheet

- Brain Awareness Week happens every year in March. The Dana Alliance for Brain Initiatives started Brain Awareness Week in 1996. The event gives students around the world the opportunity to learn more about the human brain. Scientists who study the brain tell students about their research. Students might visit museums or get the chance to look at a real human brain. This event helps children become more interested in brain health.

- Researchers found that it takes approximately 10,000 hours of focused practice for a person to become an expert at a complex skill. A complex skill could include playing a violin or playing chess. Ten thousand hours translates to approximately 10 years. But some people who have a natural talent for a skill may take less time to master it.

- Hieroglyphs written on papyrus paper in the 17th century BCE contain the first known use of the word brain. This written record comes from the ancient Egyptians. Ancient Egyptians believed that thought and emotion came from the heart. Leonardo da Vinci was the first to study the brain in great detail. He started studying human anatomy in 1506. Many new understandings of the brain came from da Vinci's experiments.

- Humans have special brain cells for socializing. These are called von Economo neurons. Neurons are brain cells that carry messages between the brain and other parts of the body. Von Economo neurons are linked to empathy and self-awareness. Humans share these neurons with only a few species of other social animals. These animals include great apes and elephants.

Glossary

adrenaline
A chemical produced by your body when you are excited, frightened, or angry.

aerobic exercise
Exercise that strengthens the heart and lungs by making them work hard for several minutes or more.

amygdala
A part of the brain that stores memories and processes emotions.

empathy
Being aware of and sharing another person's emotions.

endorphin
A chemical created by the brain that reduces pain.

glucose
A natural sugar found in plants that gives your brain energy.

hippocampus
A part of the brain that stores ideas.

hormone
A substance produced in the body that influences growth and development.

neuron
A cell that carries messages between the brain and other parts of the body.

nutrient
A substance that is needed by people to stay healthy and strong. Vitamins and minerals are nutrients.

stimulate
To make active.

stress
Worry, strain, or pressure.

For More Information

Books

DeSalle, Rob et al. *Your 21st Century Brain: Amazing Science Games to Play with Your Mind.* New York: Sterling Publishing Company, 2010.

Silver, Donald M. and Patricia J. Wynne. *My First Book about the Brain.* Mineola, NY: Dover Publications, 2013.

Swanson, Jennifer and Hank Green. *Brain Games: The Mind-Blowing Science of Your Amazing Brain.* Washington, DC: National Geographic Society, 2015.

Visit 12StoryLibrary.com

Scan the code or use your school's login at **12StoryLibrary.com** for recent updates about this topic and a full digital version of this book. Enjoy free access to:

- Digital ebook
- Breaking news updates
- Live content feeds
- Videos, interactive maps, and graphics
- Additional web resources

Note to educators: Visit 12StoryLibrary.com/register to sign up for free premium website access. Enjoy live content plus a full digital version of every 12-Story Library book you own for every student at your school.

Index

About the Author

Maddie Spalding is an enthusiastic writer and reader. She lives in Minneapolis, Minnesota. Her favorite part of writing is learning about new and interesting subjects.

READ MORE FROM 12-STORY LIBRARY

Every 12-Story Library book is available in many formats. For more information, visit 12StoryLibrary.com.